95 WAYS YOU CAN SAVE TAXES IN '95

To Bill

Please continue the good
work in the community
and thanks for being a good
friend of Bernheim. Also,
Please remember Tip #52
when thinking of Bernheim
Bob Hill
3/3/95
Charley Stivers

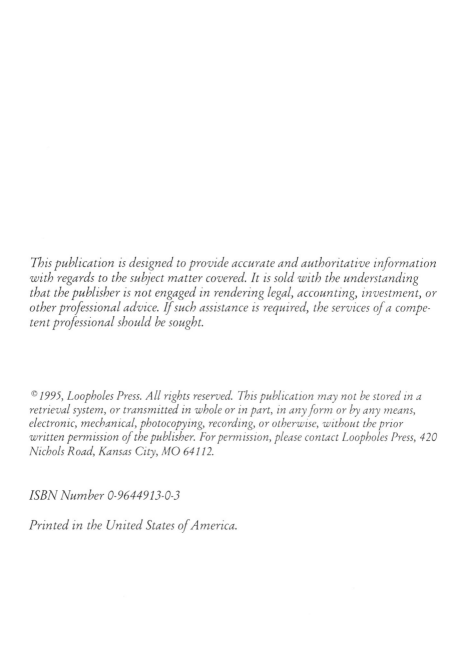

This publication is designed to provide accurate and authoritative information with regards to the subject matter covered. It is sold with the understanding that the publisher is not engaged in rendering legal, accounting, investment, or other professional advice. If such assistance is required, the services of a competent professional should be sought.

ISBN Number 0-9644913-0-3

Printed in the United States of America.

Foreword

The word "taxes" affects people in many different ways. For some people, it becomes a phobia, like a fear of flying. For others, it is as painful as a trip to the dentist. And for the remainder, it can be a confusing nuisance to be avoided at all costs.

We admit taxes are confusing and a nuisance, even painful. However, it doesn't have to be that way. Why not look at taxes as a game? Not just a game of chance, but one you can win!

That's the reason we wrote this book. We wanted to give you the rules to the game in a form you could understand and use while you have fun and save money.

If you're a game player who travels in the fast lane, this book can help you reduce your chances of being pulled over by the IRS. If you're a conservative traveler, this book can help you reach your destination by the shortest and safest route. Whatever your speed, our goal at Eskew & Gresham is to ensure you have paid the smallest entry fee and won the highest prize.

Take this book, read it, think about it. Make notes as you read it in bed at night. Call or fax your questions about it. *95 Ways You Can Save Taxes in '95* is our way of inviting you to let us coach you as you play the tax game. You'll find solid advice to help minimize your taxes. Have fun and come out a winner!

Bob Hill
(502) 584-2500 - phone
(502) 585-1647 - fax

Charley Stivers
(606) 252-6738 - phone
(606) 255-0733 - fax

95 Ways You Can Save Taxes in '95

Table Of Contents

AND

Choose A Compatible, Competent Tax Advisor

We all need first-rate help at times, and rarely so much as when we chop our way through the tax jungle. You may want to think of your accountant as a trail guide, one who not only knows where the trail leads, but makes sure that you know, too.

Find an accountant who stays current with changes in tax laws, interprets new developments, and has specific knowledge of the tax landscape.

Your accountant should inform you of obstacles and opportunities in your path, and make them clear to you. Your accountant should know your business and share your enthusiasm for your financial and business plans.

Ask a prospective accountant for references, and then ask those clients what your candidate has done for them. Ask your accountant specific questions about opportunities and pitfalls on which you may want guidance. If you get clear, informed, useful answers in an interview, you'll have found the right trail guide.

☐ Check here if you need to ask your accountant about this subject.

Notes: _____

_____

_____

_____

_____

_____

Create A Short-Term And A Long-Term Plan

Your accountant can show you before year-end how to maximize your tax savings by shifting deductions and timing your income.

What may be even more important to your future prosperity is your long-term tax plan. Your accountant will consider not only your income tax, but your estate tax, gift tax, and personal and financial goals. Your accountant can become a valued business advisor and is paid only for the services rendered. Once your plan is in place, your accountant will keep you informed about the tax law changes that can affect you in the long and short term.

For example, a law which previously denied your deduction may have changed. Your accountant will make you aware of these changes.

☐ Check here if you need to ask your accountant about this subject.

Notes: _____

_____

_____

_____

_____

_____

PERSONAL TIP
3
A N D
BUSINESS TIP
3

Soften The Punch Of New Taxes

While you are busy with work or business, your accountant is staying current with tax developments. When changes appear to threaten you with higher taxes, your accountant will not only contact you promptly with the news, but will have strategies in mind that can minimize the hit.

Timing can be essential in reducing your tax obligation. Your accountant's diligence and expertise can give you the time and knowledge you need to adjust your finances and save you from taking a tax hit.

❏ Check here if you need to ask your accountant about this subject.

Notes: _____

_____
_____
_____
_____
_____

A N D

Find Thrifty Ways
To Accumulate Money

Your accountant can show you how to make the most effective use of the full range of investment opportunities. You can maximize your return or minimize your taxes in secure investments. You can turn your investment expenses to your advantage with informed planning. Available tax-free, tax-deferred, and tax-advantaged investments can help maximize the return on your portfolio. Your accountant will help you develop an investment tax strategy that can secure a comfortable future. And, because your accountant doesn't sell investment products or profit from recommending one investment over another, you can expect the advice you get to be objective. Accountants are generally recognized as the most trustworthy independent financial advisors.

☐ Check here if you need to ask your accountant about this subject.

Notes: _____

_____

_____

_____

_____

_____

Keep Your Taxes
In The Lowest Bracket

You can't really celebrate a good year if your bounty ratchets up your tax bill. Your accountant can show you how to shelter some of your income, defer some more of it, and then show you how to take advantage of the maze of available deductions and exclusions.

Getting rich will eventually mean you are in an upper bracket, but your accountant can help you keep a larger chunk of your money in play and out of Uncle Sam's pockets.

❏ Check here if you need to ask your accountant about this subject.

Notes: _____

_____

_____

_____

_____

_____

Keep Your Record Keeping Up To Snuff

The job isn't finished until the paperwork is done, and it can seem sometimes that it will never end. You want to do business, not paperwork, and your accountant can simplify your life by advising you on the best accounting, record keeping, and inventory procedures for you and your company. If you have to cope with government licenses and contracts, your accountant can help you stay in compliance by keeping all those forms straight. Your accountant can help you choose wisely from the business or investment software available to further simplify your record keeping.

Your accountant can simplify your personal finances as well, by showing you what records you need and how to use them to your best advantage.

☐ Check here if you need to ask your accountant about this subject.

Notes: _____

_____

_____

_____

_____

_____

Get Advice On Transactions, Agreements, Claims, And Conflicts

Opportunities and obligations can take a bewildering number of forms, and can be challengingly complex in and of themselves. And when you try to figure the tax consequences, well...! Be sure of where you stand in new business ventures and in legal disputes.

A new opportunity or setback may seem complicated enough without dragging in the tax consequences of your actions. That's just when you should consider your taxes. Any agreement (legal claims,

shareholder agreements, divorce and asset sales) or transfer of property can have tax consequences that may bear on your decisions. Your accountant will make clear to you the tax consequences of the various possible outcomes, help you clarify your own thinking, and better control your position and your future. Your accountant can also handle IRS matters, such as notices and tax return examinations. Trust anyone you like, but listen to your accountant.

❏ Check here if you need to ask your accountant about this subject.

Notes: _____

_____

_____

Casualty Losses

Just when you have everything under control, trouble can come like a plague of locusts. After you have picked through the rubble and persuaded your insurance company that you weren't raising pests in the garage, you have to contend with the IRS.

The IRS recognizes sudden, unexpected, and unusual losses of property due to outside causes as casualty losses. Fire, flood, and theft are typical examples. The IRS treats personal and business casualties differently. The cost of your property, plus improvements, is reduced by the amount of insurance payments you receive. For business property, cost is always your starting point. For personal property, you start with the lesser of your cost or the fair market value of the property. (If your property retains some value, you may only deduct the loss in value.)

If a business loss, you may deduct all of the insurance shortfall. For a personal loss, the shortfall is reduced twice, first by $100 per casualty, and second by 10 percent of your adjusted gross income (AGI). You may deduct the remainder.

If your property has both personal and business uses, you may figure the deductions separately. (If your totaled car was used half the time for business, half of its basis and half of the insurance payment will be used for each computation.) NOTE: If your insurance pays more than your property's cost basis, you have a gain which may be taxable.

☐ Check here if you need to ask your accountant about this subject.

Notes: _____

_____

_____

_____

_____

_____

Disaster Losses

If the locust destruction in the surrounding area is of such a magnitude as to warrant the description of "a plague of locusts," you may have other options. Losses that occur in a Presidentially declared federal disaster area may be deducted either in the year of the loss or the previous year. In such an event, the President can be your pal no matter whom you voted for. (Though sending him or her a box of chocolates during hurricane season is NOT deductible.)

You must elect to amend your prior year's return before the due date of the loss return. If the disaster occurs late in the year, you may not have too long to make up your mind, so be sure of your figures. Differences between the two years in your adjusted gross income (AGI) and tax bracket will affect the amount of your deduction and the year you wish to claim the loss.

Keep in mind that if you deduct the loss in the year of the disaster, you may have a long wait for your refund. A refund for an amended return should arrive in about six to eight weeks.

❑ Check here if you need to ask your accountant about this subject.

Notes: _____

_____

_____

_____

_____

10 Gambling Losses

Lucky at gambling, lucky at taxes. However often your race horse placed during the year, you can deduct losses on the nags who folded. More precisely, you may deduct your gambling losses for the year, up to the amount of your gambling winnings. True, two bucks a week lost on the lottery won't shave much of anything off the zillion-dollar jackpot, but if you're that lucky – who cares? Most players are happy to stay ahead, which amounts to recovering losses and then some. The IRS only requires tax on the "then some."

Keep records of your plays, winnings, and losses, including locations, dates, and possibly names of persons present. You don't want to gamble on proving your deductions. Keep your losing tickets, etc., as well.

If you make your living as a gambler, your deductible losses probably are not limited to the amount of your winnings.

☐ Check here if you need to ask your accountant about this subject.

Notes: _____

_____

_____

_____

_____

_____

11 Property Taxes

Maybe you wonder, every time your property taxes go up, which of your neighbors voted to bleed you even drier. You'll get part of the increase back as an income tax deduction.

Your real property taxes are deductible. Special assessment "taxes" are generally not deductible, since you derive a specific benefit. Personal property taxes assessed annually on the value (and not the weight) of your property are also deductible. You cannot deduct registration, licensing, and other fees as taxes.

Deduct property taxes related to your business and rental property on the appropriate business or rental schedules. This will reduce your AGI to your greater benefit.

☐ Check here if you need to ask your accountant about this subject.

Notes: _____

_____

_____

_____

_____

12 State Tax Payments

You can save taxes by paying taxes. Let that sink in for a moment. Strange but true. Since the state taxes you pay in a year are federally deductible, the more you pay your state, the more you deduct on your federal return. Your fourth-quarter estimated tax payment is usually due to your state by January 15th. Pay that on or before December 31st and you have a larger federal deduction. Or, if you don't make estimated tax payments, you can ask your employer to withhold more state tax, and again increase your deduction.

Understand, though, that purposely overpaying the state to increase your federal deduction is specifically forbidden. You may only pay early, not extra. In effect, you're just shifting your deduction. Also, any state refund will be subject to federal tax in the year received.

Note, too, that if you are subject to alternative minimum tax, you don't benefit from paying any state or local taxes anyway. You still have to pay them, though.

☐ Check here if you need to ask your accountant about this subject.

Notes: _____

_____

_____

_____

_____

_____

PERSONAL TIP 13 Bunching Your Itemized Deductions

It's time to consider those shoeboxes full of receipts you've been meaning to organize all year. Business deductions. Personal deductions. Phase outs. Fractions! These are the things that break pencils and nerves.

The easy way out is to take the standard deduction, and that can even be to your advantage. First of all, it is the only deduction that doesn't require a cash outlay. You could think of it as free money. (Sure you can.) Second, you can bunch deductible expenses for two years into one. This can work well for certain controllable items, such as contributions, some medical expenses, or discretionary costs. Itemize for the year in which you pay all of those expenses, and take the standard deduction for the other year. Your total deduction could be significantly larger than if you itemize for both years.

Before you decide, though, consider your state return, especially if your itemized deductions roughly equal the standard deduction. If you take the federal standard deduction, most states require you to take their standard deduction, which is often less than the federal deduction.

If you itemize for the IRS, many states let you choose. Consider carefully. Most states allow deductions the IRS does not, and disallow others the IRS permits. Most states, for instance, don't allow deduction of state taxes. Figure your options, and then decide.

☐ Check here if you need to ask your accountant about this subject.

Notes: _____

_____

_____

_____

_____

_____

Tax-Related Expenses

At least the government doesn't expect you to chop your way through the tax jungle without assistance. Most of the attorney's fees, court costs, and other legal expenses incurred by your business are deductible, including fees for tax advice and litigation. Capital expenditures and personal legal expenses are not deductible through your business. Neither are expenses for acquiring, perfecting, or defending your title to property. (These are added to the cost of the property.)

On your personal return, you may deduct as miscellaneous expenses all of your ordinary and necessary legal expenses related to the determination, collection, or refund of any tax imposed on you by any level of government, or by any foreign government.

Personal legal expense outside this definition is generally not deductible. For instance, no expenses related to tax-free income are deductible. Additionally, divorcing persons may not deduct fees for the divorce. However, they may deduct legal fees for tax advice related to the divorce.

☐ Check here if you need to ask your accountant about this subject.

Notes: _____

_____

_____

_____

_____

_____

15 Business Transportation

You have to get to work to go to work, but the feds don't consider ordinary commuting expenses deductible. However, if you travel once you get to work, you can deduct the related expenses. All cab, bus, train, airfares, and automotive expenses incurred in the conduct of business are deductible.

Additionally, if you work in more than one location during the day, you can deduct the costs of traveling from one site to another. This includes driving between your primary job and a second job. If you receive a temporary assignment at a location outside your own general area, you can deduct the costs of daily round trips from your home.

If you have deductible auto expenses, you generally may either record and deduct your actual expenses, including depreciation, or record your mileage and deduct at the business rate. (This was 29¢ per mile for 1994.) In a few instances, use of the mileage rate is prohibited. If you deduct according to your mileage, you may also deduct your parking and toll fees, though no other actual costs.

No matter which way you go, remember you can deduct auto expenses only for the conduct of business. If your employer reimburses you for travel, the reimbursement is not usually included in your income, and you don't deduct the expenses. Expenses for which you are not reimbursed are deductible as miscellaneous itemized deductions, subject to the 2 percent of adjusted gross income (AGI) limit.

☐ Check here if you need to ask your accountant about this subject.

Notes: _____

_____

_____

_____

_____

16 · Nonbusiness Bad Debts

When cousin Larry stops showing up for family picnics and gets an unlisted number, you may get the idea you are never going to see that $500 you loaned him for his dental work. Or was it patio furniture?

If you expected to be repaid and can demonstrate that you no longer expect to be, you can deduct the loan as a short-term capital loss. Your main concern is that the IRS may consider your loan a gift, especially if you made it to a friend or family member. So get a note acknowledging the debt and reasonable interest when you make such a loan, and be prepared to prove that the debtor is unable to pay you back. A filing for bankruptcy will do the trick, but you may need no more than a letter from Larry saying he won't repay you. If you can't find him, that in itself may constitute proof of default.

So what were you thinking when you wrote that check, you old softie?

☐ Check here if you need to ask your accountant about this subject.

Notes: _____

_____

_____

_____

Interest Deductions

Deductions for interest payments can make getting into debt almost attractive. Qualifying interest is deductible so long as it is actually paid on a true, demonstrable debt during the tax year. Even usurious rates of interest fully qualify. Interest on business debt is fully deductible. Interest on a qualified residential mortgage is fully deductible. Interest on a loan used for investment is deductible up to specific limits (discussed later). Interest expenses for income from certain passive activities may be deductible, subject to certain criteria and limits. (Get help on this one.)

Ah, the exceptions. Personal interest is probably not deductible. That would be the credit card interest or the 5 percent you pay your brother for bailing you out on your speedboat payments. Interest paid on a loan used to purchase tax-exempt securities is not deductible. Any unconventional indebtedness should be reviewed by your accountant, who can determine if interest paid is deductible.

☐ Check here if you need to ask your accountant about this subject.

Notes: _____

_____

_____

_____

_____

_____

PERSONAL TIP

18

Medical Deductions

You can be sure you will still have medical bills to pay, and all indications are they will continue to be deductible, although the rules may change a little. Then as now, you should take every deduction you can.

For the present, only your medical and dental expenses in excess of 7.5 percent of your adjusted gross income (AGI) are deductible. So if you and yours are in the pink, you may get no deduction. Further, the insurance reimbursements you receive reduce your potential deduction.

You may wish to maximize your deduction by bunching medical bills into one year. If you can delay one major procedure into next year, when you expect to have others, you may be able to deduct more of your medical expenses. Or perhaps you can reschedule next year's procedures into this year.

Deductible expenses run the gamut between medical and dental insurance premiums (including Medicare Part B), prescriptions, fees for consultation and services, costs of corrective equipment like eyeglasses, wheelchairs, and prostheses, costs of medically necessary home improvements such as ramps and filtering equipment, any hospital bills you pay, and costs of residential facilities, including special needs schools that are entered for medical reasons.

You may have a medical bill that doesn't seem to appear on any list of eligible deductions. Your accountant should be familiar with the current eligibility listings. Ask – we haven't listed everything.

☐ Check here if you need to ask your accountant about this subject.

Notes: _____

_____

_____

_____

_____

_____

Investment Expenses

Now, as always, it takes money to make money. And the IRS allows you to deduct your ordinary and necessary investment expenses as an itemized deduction, subject to certain limitations. These expenses include costs of research, including relevant subscriptions and professional advice, and security measures such as safe deposit boxes. Remember that you can't deduct expenses related to tax-exempt investments.

Some expenses are not treated as deductions. For example, stockbroker's fees are treated as adjustments to your sale price. If the sale of a property requires advertising, legal fees, title insurance, or other instruments, these are also adjustments to your sale price.

Your accountant should know what fees and expenses to look for and will help you maximize your deductions and adjustments. Your deductible investment expenses are subject to a 2 percent adjusted gross income limitation.

☐ Check here if you need to ask your accountant about this subject.

Notes: _____

_____

_____

_____

_____

_____

20 Appreciated Property

Investment properties can give you considerable control over your eventual wealth and current tax losses. A property that appreciates in value while paying little or no income to you is not taxable until you sell the property. You can delay selling such a property until a year in which your tax rate is low. You can even give a property to your children, who may sell it and be taxed at their lower rate. (Be sure to consider any potential gift tax.)

Further, while income-producing investments are taxed at regular rates (as high as 39.6 percent), profit from a property sale could be taxed as a long-term capital gain (for which the maximum rate is 28 percent). Thus, a property that appreciates at 5 percent per year may produce more wealth for you than does another investment that pays 7 percent interest.

Consider other costs before you commit to such an investment. Broker's fees, closing costs, and property taxes, among others, can reduce your eventual gain. And remember, too, that not every cow pasture or painting by a Frenchman is going to appreciate.

☐ Check here if you need to ask your accountant about this subject.

Notes: _____

_____

_____

_____

_____

_____

PERSONAL TIP

21 Capital Gains

Many investments pay some sort of income to you, while at the same time increase in value. (Here's hoping!) Investment income (interest, dividends, etc.) is usually taxed at your regular rate. You don't profit from an investment's increase in value until you sell it, and that profit is called capital gain. If you lose money on the sale, you have a capital loss.

Capital gains are taxed differently than regular income. Short-term gains (from investments held one year or less) are taxed at your regular rate. Long-term gains (held more than a year) are taxed at a maximum rate of 28 percent. And you can offset your gains with your losses. Subtract your short-term losses from your short-term gains. Subtract your long-term losses from your long-term gains. If either remainder is negative, subtract it from the other. A positive remainder (your net capital gain) is taxed at the appropriate rate. That is, if your net gain is from a short-term investment, your regular rate applies. If your net gain is long-term, the lower, long-term rate applies. Try to hold investments to take advantage of this lower 28 percent rate.

If you have a net loss up to $3,000, you can deduct it. Losses over $3,000 carry over to future years to offset future gains.

Look at where you stand before year-end. If you have a net capital loss, consider selling to generate a capital gain (or vice versa).

☐ Check here if you need to ask your accountant about this subject.

Notes: _____

_____

_____

_____

_____

_____

Long-Term Capital Gains As Investment Income

Here's a choice you didn't have until 1993. Long-term capital gains used to be included in regular investment income. Now they are considered separately, at their lower tax rate, unless you choose to lump them back in at the higher, regular rate.

Why do such a thing? If your net investment income is less than your investment interest expenses, you may want to include your long-term capital gains in your investment income. In this way, you can reap the benefit of the balance of your interest expense deduction. Even if this means a higher tax rate applies to your capital gains, your larger expense deduction may result in greater effective savings.

Before making this decision, consider that you can carry over any excess investment interest expense to a later year, provided you will have investment income to offset.

☐ Check here if you need to ask your accountant about this subject.

Notes: _____

_____

_____

_____

_____

_____

23 Certificates Of Deposit

They aren't sexy and they won't balloon into millions, but CDs are generally safe and reliable. The rate of return is often lower than for other investments, but it is guaranteed, and most CDs are government-insured. Usually, the longer the term of the CD, the higher the rate of return. Just remember that withdrawing money from a CD prematurely may result in a penalty.

You should plan for the taxes you will have to pay on your CD earnings. If, in mid-year, you buy a one-year CD, you will owe no taxes until the CD matures. If, on the other hand, you buy a three-month CD and continue to roll it over for a one-year period, you will owe taxes on interest earned in each year the CD is active.

If you are an accrual basis taxpayer (such as most businesses), this deferral won't work.

☐ Check here if you need to ask your accountant about this subject.

Notes: _____

_____

_____

_____

_____

_____

Employee Stock Ownership Plans (ESOPs)

Ever dream your boss worked for you? Or that you owned the place? Many small, closely held firms are finding that these dreams make good business sense. An ESOP is a retirement plan that invests in company stock for employees. On departure or retirement, an employee receives his or her share of stock as a nest egg. Dividends paid along the way are distributed among the accounts of active employees.

Federal policy encourages ESOPs. This makes them appealing, but it also means that policy guidelines, which change frequently, must be met. Also, a family-owned company may resist sharing control, though most ESOPs vote their shares through a management appointee. Still, the advantages are clear for both the employer and employee.

An ESOP's advantage is that the seller may defer the gain on the sale of stock to the plan. Even borrowing money to purchase the stock may generate favorable tax treatment.

☐ Check here if you need to ask your accountant about this subject.

Notes: _____

_____

_____

_____

_____

_____

Installment Sales

What could be nicer than selling an investment or business asset for a big profit? What could be worse than paying all those taxes on the profits? What to do?

An installment sale is a possible answer. You can contract with your buyer to receive a down payment in the first year and installment payments, with interest, in subsequent years. The IRS allows you to pay tax on your gain in the year you receive the money rather than paying it all in the year of sale. However, assets which have been depreciated may result in some gain in the year of sale, even if there is no down payment. Plan the timing of payments to make sure you have the cash to pay tax on this gain.

If you have held the property for more than a year, rates for long-term capital gains may apply. The interest you receive is taxed as regular income in the year you receive it.

☐ Check here if you need to ask your accountant about this subject.

Notes: _____

_____

_____

_____

_____

_____

26 Investment Interest

When a hot investment opportunity comes along, you may be tempted to borrow money to get in on it. Doubters may warn you how risky and irresponsible that would be, but the opportunity might be sound and create a tremendous possibility for you.

The interest on your loan is generally deductible, unless the loan is for a tax-exempt investment. You can deduct all of your interest up to the total of your net investment income (investment income less investment expenses). You may carry any interest deductions in excess of that maximum forward to future years, when your investment income is greater than your interest expense.

Investigate the details thoroughly, and if it still looks good, go out and make a fortune.

☐ Check here if you need to ask your accountant about this subject.

Notes: _____

_____

_____

_____

_____

_____

Options

Buying options is much like kids playing dibs. An option is a contract that secures your right to buy or sell an investment for a set price on a set date. Options are bought and sold on real property, as well as on stocks and securities, for varied reasons. Suppose you wish to raise money for a purchase. Buy an option to secure this opportunity through the date you expect to be ready. A seller may buy an option to secure a certain price for a later sale date. Daredevil investors buy and sell options like stock, looking for a profitable difference between the fixed price and the property's actual value at date of sale.

You can use options in several ways to keep your taxes down. If, for example, you intend to sell property and don't want to report the gain this year, sell an option on it. When you close the sale next year, you will have postponed your gain and your tax obligation.

Some option strategies are sensible, low-risk investments, while others can and do result in big losses. So long as you are careful and know what you're doing, you can use them to great advantage.

☐ Check here if you need to ask your accountant about this subject.

Notes: _____

_____

_____

_____

_____

_____

28   Real Estate Investments

Despite short-term fluctuations, the old cliche is generally true: Land is a safe, secure, and profitable investment. The one necessity is to acquire property at the right price. An inflated price may eventually produce a gain, but it might take a lifetime to see your investment pay off.

Educate yourself about market prices and trends, and seek professional guidance. Keep comprehensive records of all your costs, most of which will adjust your taxable gain to your advantage when you sell. Discuss your depreciation options with your accountant.

Many real estate investments are subject to the complicated "passive activity loss" (PAL) rules, because they are usually rental properties or real estate partnerships. Several strategies can maximize your return. Generally, if one of your real estate properties produces a tax loss, income from similar property you buy will be yours tax-free, as long as your unused losses at least equal your income or gain. Simply changing your level of involvement with the property can change its classification and reap a tax advantage.

In any case, a good price on property is the best reason to buy if you are looking for sound investments. Considerable returns will be yours when the property appreciates, and you won't owe a dime of tax on the appreciation until you choose to sell.

☐ Check here if you need to ask your accountant about this subject.

Notes: _____

_____

_____

_____

_____

_____

Investing In Small Business – You're A Winner!

If you pick a winner, and a little shop with a good idea grows your money like so much cabbage, you can further increase your net gain if your stock met certain requirements upon issue. The 1993 Revenue Reconciliation Act added two money-saving provisions.

One provision excludes from tax half of your gain from the sale of stock. This applies only to stock in certain industries, and you must hold the stock for at least five years to qualify. If you are looking at new businesses as potential investments, or if you plan a new division or product line in your own business, look into the stock requirements. You might save a bundle later.

The other provision allows you to defer some or all of your gain from sale of publicly traded stock if you reinvest in a "specialized small business investment company."

Ask your accountant for details.

❑ Check here if you need to ask your accountant about this subject.

Notes: _____

_____

_____

_____

_____

_____

Investing In Small Business – You're A Loser!

Perhaps you dream of getting in on the ground floor, putting your money behind an inventor or visionary who will take your money through the roof. It happens. Some of our modern computer or industrial giants started in a garage or basement, and their early investors have done very well, thank you.

However, more often than not, the ground floor falls into the basement. All you'll have left are memories and tax problems, unless the investment you choose qualifies you for a break.

In most cases, your individual deduction for net capital losses is limited to $3,000 per year. However, this limit does not apply to what is called "Section 1244" stock. This category was created to encourage investment in small business. Losses under Section 1244 are deductible as ordinary losses up to $50,000 per individual, or $100,000 for a joint return. A new business may be willing to meet Section 1244 requirements in order to attract and protect your investment. Your accountant can determine whether the stock qualifies.

☐ Check here if you need to ask your accountant about this subject.

Notes: _____

_____

_____

_____

_____

_____

Rollover Of Gain – SSBIC

If part of your portfolio is ripe to sell, but in the process you'll face severe tax consequences, you may want to invest part of your gain in a Specialized Small Business Investment Company (SSBIC). You can roll over gain from the sale of publicly traded securities into an SSBIC. The IRS allows you to defer tax on this gain.

The Small Business Administration licenses SSBICs. Plus, Uncle Sam encourages you to invest in them, to certain limits. Only regular corporations (C) and individuals may invest with this advantage. You'll have to purchase common stock or a partnership interest in an SSBIC during the 60 days following the gainful sale of the securities. A word of caution, though. There's a maximum gain you may roll over into an SSBIC. Be sure you consult your accountant about these limits.

☐ Check here if you need to ask your accountant about this subject.

Notes: _____

_____

_____

_____

_____

_____

32 401(k)s

Wouldn't a raise be great? How about a tax cut? Hey, why not both? That's what a 401(k) plan can offer. This is a stock bonus or profit sharing plan created by an employer. You can defer a portion of your salary (up to the lesser of 15 percent of salary or a cap, which is a little over $9,000 per year) into a 401(k). Some employers opt to match a portion of employee contributions. Your tax obligation on your contribution is deferred until you receive money from the plan.

The employer's contribution will be distributed according to the plan's vesting schedule, which you will want to examine. If you leave employment before vesting, you won't receive the employer's contributed amount. Not every employee will benefit from the employer's contribution, though you will receive all of your own contributed funds and their earnings.

You can think of employer contributions as a raise you invest toward retirement. Since you are not taxed on total contributions until you receive the money, which will likely be after you retire, the tax rate applied will probably be lower than your present rate. In any case, you avoid current tax on both your contributions and earnings on your 401(k) account.

☐ Check here if you need to ask your accountant about this subject.

Notes: _____

_____

_____

_____

_____

_____

Individual Retirement Accounts (IRAs)

Anybody can create a retirement plan, and its name is IRA. You can invest a maximum of $2,000 per year (a combined amount of $2,250 if one spouse is not working) in an IRA, and taxes on the earnings are deferred until you withdraw money, so your nest egg grows all the faster. If neither you nor your spouse are enrolled in an employer's retirement plan, or you're covered by your employer's plan but your income is below certain maximums, you can also deduct your contributions. You can lower your taxes every year while you save.

Penalties apply if you withdraw money before you are 59½. Still, if you leave your deductible contributions alone for five to 10 years, (somewhat longer for nondeductible contributions), your account, even after penalties, may be larger than an equivalent taxable account would be. You just have to work the numbers, based on what earnings rate you can get. IRAs work, and the government created them. Ponder that one for a moment.

You can contribute to your IRA until April 15 of the following year and still claim your allowable deduction. But you can't start earning until you invest. The earlier in the year you invest, the better the return.

❑ Check here if you need to ask your accountant about this subject.

Notes: _____

_____

_____

_____

_____

_____

34 Nonqualified Plans

If your employer is secure and thriving, consider signing up for a nonqualified deferred compensation plan. Through such a plan, your employer agrees to pay you later for your current services. You postpone receipt of compensation until retirement, when you will be in a lower tax bracket. You owe tax only when you receive the money, or when you acquire an unrestricted right to it.

Such a plan is "nonqualified" because it doesn't meet the more strict requirements of qualified pension plans. There is some risk to you, because money in the plan remains vulnerable to your employer's creditors. Research your company's health and long-term prospects before signing up.

☐ Check here if you need to ask your accountant about this subject.

Notes: _____

_____

_____

_____

_____

_____

PERSONAL TIP

35 Qualified Retirement Plans

Your employer's pension or profit sharing plan is a Qualified Retirement Plan. This is a deferred compensation plan with your share, and your earnings on that amount, withheld until you leave the company or retire. You pay no taxes on your portion until you receive the money. A pension plan typically defines your eventual benefit amount according to your wages and tenure. A profit sharing plan typically defines the employer's contribution annually, with your ultimate benefit amount determined by the size and earnings of your share of the contributions.

A qualified plan usually defines (in a vesting schedule) the lump sum you receive if you leave prior to retirement. If you plan to leave, you will want to know how much you are vested, and how much longer you need to stay to get another year's vesting. If your new employer has a qualified plan, you can roll over your vested earnings into it and avoid paying taxes on the money until retirement.

Other rules and advantages may apply to your plan. Study the snappy brochure your employer provides, and ask questions. If your employer doesn't have a plan, shower him with encouragement to establish one. And, consider taking advantage of an IRA.

☐ Check here if you need to ask your accountant about this subject.

Notes: ______________________________

____

____

____

____

____

Retirement Plans: Planning And Distribution

Keoghs, IRAs, profit sharing – if you are fortunate enough to have a choice, the decision can seem mind-bending. Making the right choice is worth it, though. A retirement plan may be your best tax shelter. Keep in mind that most plans have some rules in common. Most, for instance, don't allow withdrawals before age 59½ without a tax penalty. Inconvenient, perhaps, but this inaccessibility means you won't be taxed on your money until you do withdraw it. Some plans will allow penalty-free loans before that age, provided they are repaid within a certain time, usually short-term.

Perhaps your main concern is the limit on your contribution. An IRA is limited to $2,000 per person per year ($4,000 for a married couple filing jointly), while a profit sharing plan is limited to contribution equal to 15 percent of eligible compensation, of which your annual portion might be greater than $2,000. A money purchase plan limits contributions to 25 percent of compensation in combination with profit sharing. If your employer is particularly profitable and secure, such a plan could be well worth developing, if you don't have one already.

If you are self-employed, you have a number of options your accountant can outline for you.

☐ Check here if you need to ask your accountant about this subject.

Notes: _____

_____

_____

_____

_____

_____

Mutual Funds

If you know you're not a financial wizard, but simply want one to manage your investments, you might consider mutual funds. Many investors pool their resources in these diversified portfolios managed by market professionals. Returns are generally higher than from savings accounts or CDs, and diversification provides a measure of security.

Mutual funds are as varied as the market itself. Some invest in common stock, some in international markets, some in tax-exempt securities. Naturally, some are more successful than others, and some will even lose money. Listen to the experience of others, but do your own research before you choose a fund. As with most investments, your money will be at risk.

Earnings from mutual funds come in varied forms and are treated differently, and favorably, by the IRS. Earnings may be ordinary or tax-free dividends, realized or undistributed capital gains, or nontaxable return of capital. The company managing your funds will identify any earnings, and usually will advise you in general about applicable tax rules.

Sales of fund shares are treated like regular stock sales; you may specifically identify the shares sold, or you may choose one of two methods to average the cost of shares you sell to determine your taxable gain. This option applies only to mutual funds, and, if you choose to average your costs, you must always use the same method for that fund.

☐ Check here if you need to ask your accountant about this subject.

Notes: _____

_____

_____

_____

_____

_____

Savings Bonds – U.S.

Some people won't even consider these bonds. Kid stuff, they say. They are right in a way, but what a deal the kids get! They are sold for less than face value and may be redeemed at set intervals for set amounts. You always know where you are with government Savings Bonds. The increase in value over the purchase price is reported as interest income on your tax return.

For most bonds, you can choose whether to report your earnings each year or at redemption. Your kids can make out here. Earnings from Savings Bonds in your child's name are sheltered by a $600 standard deduction. Once the child is old enough to incur a tax obligation and redeems the bonds, the interest protected by the deduction over the years comes whole and untaxed.

If your child is under 14 and subject to your marginal tax rate, you can defer reporting the interest until he is older and can avoid paying marginal tax. This works for older folks, too, who often defer reporting Savings Bond interest until they retire and their tax rate drops.

If you redeem Series EE bonds purchased after 1989 for the higher education expenses of your immediate family, you can exclude the interest from your taxable income. You may be able to exclude interest you actually spend on education. The exclusion is phased out above certain income levels. Still, what a deal!

☐ Check here if you need to ask your accountant about this subject.

Notes: _____

_____

_____

_____

_____

_____

39   Worthless Securities

Well, how were you supposed to know that Mutant Housepets, Inc., would fizzle? MHI is in some lawyer's bottom drawer now, and the wizards you banked on to lead the company are nowhere to be found.

Seek wisdom from the experience, and deduct your investment as a capital loss. (Some small business stocks can be deducted as ordinary losses.) The loss is considered to have occurred on Dec. 31st of the year the stock becomes worthless. So, always look over your portfolio before year-end. Identify stock which may be worthless, and check it out.

You must be able to demonstrate the stock is without value. If the company declares bankruptcy, or if it or its officers disappear without forwarding addresses, you probably meet this requirement.

If you weren't paying attention, and your stock folded in one of the last seven years, you can amend that year's return. This is more generous than the general rule limiting amendment of returns to the last three years.

☐ Check here if you need to ask your accountant about this subject.

Notes: _____

_____

_____

_____

_____

40 Short Sales

Sell someone the Brooklyn Bridge and they'll call you a crook. Sell stock you don't own and they'll just call you short. A short sale is a way to make money in a falling market. In effect, you borrow stock from your broker to sell at the current price, and then later replace it with stock you buy at, hopefully, a lower price.

Because you don't complete the transaction until you present your broker with stock in payment, you can sell short this year, buy the lower-priced stock next year, and defer tax obligations on the deal until next year.

It sounds rosy, but please remember that stocks have been known to increase in value, even when we don't want them to. You can lose money.

☐ Check here if you need to ask your accountant about this subject.

Notes: _____

_____

_____

_____

_____

_____

41 Tax-Exempt Bonds

What a pretty idea. It's practically free money. States and municipalities issue bonds for various public works projects, essentially borrowing for construction what they expect to gain in increased tax revenue. The interest on these securities is usually not federally taxable. It may be subject to alternative minimum tax (AMT) or cause some of your Social Security benefits to be taxed. Your own state usually will not tax bonds issued within its borders. Usually, your state will tax bond earnings from other states.

The interest rate on tax-exempt bonds is lower than on taxable securities, but the tax advantage can mean greater net earnings. For example, if you are in the 36 percent tax bracket and purchase 6 percent municipal bonds, your earnings are equivalent to those, after taxes, from an investment paying 9.4 percent.

☐ Check here if you need to ask your accountant about this subject.

Notes: _____

_____

_____

_____

_____

_____

42 Taxable Bonds

The bond market can seem bewildering enough to intimidate the most stout-hearted, but there is money to be made, and lost, here. Companies issue bonds to raise capital. Investors are like the issuer's bankers. Their investments are loans, repaid with interest.

You first should learn something about the variety of bonds available, and then about the bond rating system, which indicates the relative safety of an investment. A triple A rating, the highest, indicates that a bond issuer is very secure and stable. Less secure bonds generally offer a temptingly higher rate of return, but issuers have been known to default. Consider carefully what you can afford to risk. Zero-coupon bonds can be a very attractive investment. They pay no cash interest. Instead, earnings are reinvested at the same rate and compounded. Because of this, zero-coupon bonds are sold for a price far below their face value.

Zero-coupon bonds are often good long-term investments. The greatest drawback is that the earnings are taxable annually, even though the investor receives no cash. However, bonds purchased through a tax-exempt Keogh or IRA avoid taxation until the account is tapped.

☐ Check here if you need to ask your accountant about this subject.

Notes: _____

_____

_____

_____

_____

_____

Wash Sales

What if you sold stock you own at a loss, then bought the same stock? You'd have a capital loss to deduct, and still have your capital. Pretty slick, eh? Especially at year-end when you may want more loss to reduce your taxes.

It's called a wash sale, and that sound you hear is the IRS waggling its finger at you. They don't like it when you claim a loss and haven't actually lost anything. You can still make a wash sale, but the IRS has written certain restrictions on their deductibility. Mainly, you have to buy the equivalent stock more than 30 days before or 30 days after you sell your stock, or you can't claim the loss on the sale.

Even so, if you repurchase within these 61 days, you can still add the loss to the basis of your repurchased stock. This will reduce your profits, on paper at least, when you sell the stock, and reduce your tax obligation.

☐ Check here if you need to ask your accountant about this subject.

Notes: _____

_____

_____

_____

_____

_____

PERSONAL TIP 44

Buying And Selling Stock

Buy low, sell high. It's hard to go wrong following advice like that. Some do, though, come tax time, for lack of foresight. If, for instance, you expect to realize large capital gains soon, you should consider how long you've held the stock and whether you will be in a different tax bracket this year than next. Generally, you want to sell your stock in the year you are in the lower bracket. Sell failing stock in the same year to realize losses that will reduce your taxable gain. You may want simply to hold your stock for a year or more in order to qualify for the 28 percent maximum long-term capital gains rate, especially if you are in a higher bracket.

If your tax rate is better next year than this, but you expect your stock to decline in value by then, you can secure your gain by either selling short or buying an option to sell your shares, so that the transaction is completed next year.

You can claim up to $3,000 in capital losses each year and reduce your taxable income. Still, you may not want to sell shares that are only temporarily in decline, and you may not want to risk losses in a wash sale. Consider selling the shares and buying comparable stock in a similar company.

☐ Check here if you need to ask your accountant about this subject.

Notes: _____

_____

_____

_____

_____

_____

PERSONAL TIP 45

Gifts To Family Members

Gift and estate taxes can take as much as 55 percent of funds you transfer to others, but there are ways to avoid much of the tax liability. Anyone can give up to $10,000 to an unlimited number of recipients each year tax-free, and a married couple can give $20,000 per recipient. You can make such gifts directly or through a trust that controls the principal. Many estates can be completely transferred in this way over time.

Gifts to your spouse who is an American citizen escape all taxation. If your spouse is not a citizen, certain rules limit the amount of gifts and the manner of transfer. However, these gifts do not eliminate estate tax when the property later transfers. To limit tax liability, you can set up two or more asset pools, for your spouse and for your children, that can be protected from tax under separate rules.

☐ Check here if you need to ask your accountant about this subject.

Notes: _____

_____

_____

_____

_____

_____

Estate Taxes

That inescapable day will come, and your family will certainly find comfort in your sensible plans to preserve your estate for their security. Your first tool in planning your bequests is the automatic federal credit for the first $192,800 in transfer taxes, which amounts to a tax exclusion for the first $600,000 of your estate. This is in addition to the annual exclusion for gifts of $10,000.

The spousal exclusion for gifts described earlier also applies to bequests. So, you can transfer a substantial estate to your spouse tax-free. However, at death, each of you can pass only $600,000 to your children (or other heirs) tax-free.

A federal generation-skipping tax can take as much as 55 percent from bequests to your grandchildren, after you bequeath an excludable maximum total of $1,000,000. This is in addition to regular estate taxes on amounts above $600,000.

Keep your bequests from falling into the government's hands by transferring portions of your estate into your family's hands now. The exclusion of $600,000 may seem like a lot of money, but 20 or 30 years from now, your property may be worth a lot more than that.

☐ Check here if you need to ask your accountant about this subject.

Notes: _____

_____

_____

_____

_____

_____

Secrets Of "Success"ion Planning

Suppose you spent the last 28 years building and managing your business. Now, you dream of passing the business to someone else, curling up inside the Sponge Bar on Grand Bahama and writing your life story.

With the right amount of planning, you can keep the bucks rolling in without showing up for work every day. But you'll need to be a savvy planner.

When defining your succession plan, consider one of several options.

1. You can pass the business and future growth to your children or other relatives.

2. You can sell the company or transfer it through some type of nontaxable reorganization.

3. You can transfer the ownership to one or more employees.

As you analyze your options, also consider your family's long-term plans for the business. The success of your retirement is dependent upon the strength of your business plan, your estate plan, and the advice you receive.

☐ Check here if you need to ask your accountant about this subject.

Notes: _____

_____

_____

_____

_____

_____

Other Estate Transfer Planning Strategies

If your estate will exceed the excludable $600,000, it remains a good idea to make $10,000 annual gifts over time or to look into the variety of trusts you may establish that can ensure an income stream to your loved ones. It depends on what you want. If, for example, you want to choose who receives your assets after your spouse's death, you can establish a qualified terminable interest property trust (QTIP). A QTIP pays its income to your surviving spouse, with the remainder going to the person of your choice after your spouse's death.

Many choose life insurance policies as safe and reliable means to provide for their survivors. Just remember that the proceeds are subject to estate tax if payable to your estate. You can transfer a policy to certain trusts at least three years before you die or give money to the trust to buy the policy. The proceeds will be tax-free, though your initial gift, and the premiums you pay, may be subject to gift tax.

Consult with your accountant about these and other available options.

☐ Check here if you need to ask your accountant about this subject.

Notes: _____

_____

_____

_____

_____

_____

49 Employ Your Children

It's the way things used to be; everyone in the family doing his or her part to make the family business go. Think of the old farmstead or the corner candy store. Think of the Ewings of *Dallas*. Well, OK, there are some risks. But if you have a business and can legitimately employ your children, several tax advantages are yours.

First, of course, your child's wages are fully deductible as a business expense. Also, if you are a sole proprietor, you need not pay FICA on those wages until an employed child turns 18, or unemployment insurance until the child turns 21.

Also, consider that your child's wages are subject to a lower tax rate than if you retain the same money as business earnings. The money is still in the family, and there's more of it.

Also, a child with earned income receives a standard deduction of $3,800 for 1994 (1995 will be close to $3,900) and qualifies for an IRA deduction of $2,000. So, about $6,000 of your child's earnings can be tax-free. Go ahead, introduce your children to the world of business.

☐ Check here if you need to ask your accountant about this subject.

Notes: _____

_____

_____

_____

_____

_____

Shift Income To Your Children

Certainly there are other reasons to have children, but they can be great little tax shelters, too. Children 14 and over pay a modest 15 percent on earned and unearned income up to $22,750 in 1994. (The amount will be somewhat higher for 1995.) Since you are in a higher bracket, consider shifting some investments into your child's name. However, don't forget about alternative minimum tax consequences to your child.

A taxpayer can give each of any number of recipients up to $10,000 tax-free each year. The limit for a married couple is $20,000. Over time, you can shift substantial investments to your child, which will reduce your present tax liability and estate tax liability when you die.

If you are leery of giving your child access to all that capital, you can set up several kinds of trusts that pay income and protect the principal, at least until age 21.

☐ Check here if you need to ask your accountant about this subject.

Notes: _____

_____

_____

_____

_____

_____

51 Donate Assets

What could be nicer than to profit from your own generosity? A charitable remainder trust allows you to donate property to a charity (through the trust) and receive an annuity for a period of years. Any remaining earnings and the principal go to the charity, and you get a tax deduction in the year you make the contribution. If the trust sells the property, it pays no capital gains tax. Subsequent earnings are greater than if you had sold the property, since the full amount can be invested. After the annuity period, the capital and earnings go to the charity. This strategy is especially effective for highly appreciated property which generates little or no current earnings, such as land. You get a deduction, generate an income stream, and receive the charity benefits, too.

Some charities offer pooled income funds that work in the same way and have the strength of multiple donations to secure and improve earnings. It is also allowable to donate your home, with the provision that you may live in it until you die. You receive a deduction in the year of donation.

❒ Check here if you need to ask your accountant about this subject.

Notes: _____

_____

_____

_____

_____

_____

52 Appreciated And Depreciated Property

Here's an easy one. Give appreciated property to charity for a tax advantage. Don't give depreciated property to charity.

Here's the advantage. If you sell appreciated property and then donate the proceeds, you have to pay the tax on your profit from the sale. This reduces the amount of money you can give to charity. You get a contribution deduction for the net amount given to charity. If you give the property directly, you're not taxed on the appreciation. The charity gets more money

because they can sell the property and not pay tax. You get a contribution deduction for the value of the property.

If you sell depreciated property and donate the proceeds, you may be able to deduct both your capital loss and your contribution. If you give the property directly, you have no loss to deduct, though you still get your charitable deduction for the value of the property.

There is a complicated option. (You knew it, didn't you?) You can sell appreciated property to a charity for part of its value and recover all or part of your cost. Such transfers are treated as part sale and part contribution. Your savings are less than for a direct gift, but you get some cash.

☐ Check here if you need to ask your accountant about this subject.

Notes: _____
_____
_____
_____

Cash And Noncash Contributions

Cash contributions to qualified charities are deductible for the year in which you make them, so long as you receive nothing in return. If you receive something, a meal or unique craft item, you reduce your deduction by the value of it. By law, the charity has to tell you its value. (Don't be disappointed.) Remember, you must get a receipt for every donation of $250 or more to one charity. Your cancelled check will suffice for smaller amounts.

You cannot deduct time you work for a charity, though your attendant expenses are deductible. Deduct 12 cents per mile for any driving you do for the charity in your car.

You may deduct items you donate to a rummage sale or charity auction at their fair market value. What would you pay for them, charitable impulses aside? It's a good idea to document your property donations, and perhaps even to photograph them, in case questions arise.

To deduct property donations worth more than $500, you must provide more information with your return. If an item other than stock is worth more than $5,000, you must have it appraised to deduct it. If nonpublic stock you donate is worth more than $10,000, it must also be appraised. In addition to your tax savings, you are fully entitled to that rosy glow of fellowship.

❏ Check here if you need to ask your accountant about this subject.

Notes: _____

_____

_____

_____

_____

_____

Business Contributions – Inventory

You can't stay in business by giving away your inventory. But sometimes a donation of inventory reaps a deduction greater than your purchase cost. If your company has a policy of giving to others, and you have inventory of use to the poor, the sick, or infants, the government offers you some additional incentives to keep up the good work.

Your company may, for example, contribute food and medical supplies from inventory to a qualified charity, who will use the materials to provide for the homeless. You then may deduct not only the cost of the goods, but half of the lost profit as well.

To take advantage of this deduction, your company must be a C corporation.

☐ Check here if you need to ask your accountant about this subject.

Notes: _____

_____

_____

_____

_____

_____

55 Cafeteria Plans

Go ahead – take the donut. If your employer offers a cafeteria benefit plan, you'll want your blood sugar up and a clear mind, because you have some choices to make. Choice is the point and the advantage of a cafeteria plan.

Under such a plan, you may choose from a smorgasbord of benefit options offered by your employer. Medical insurance, dental insurance, certain life insurance, medical expenses, and dependent care may be on the list. For tax purposes, you will want to distinguish between options that pay cash to you and those that don't. Cash you receive is taxable, regardless of what it is called. Under the cafeteria plan, your employer offers the option of reducing your salary in exchange for a nontaxable benefit, such as payment of medical expenses. Your medical expenses are then paid with pretax dollars. This will also reduce your tax liability. Go back for the cherry cobbler, look over the plan's descriptive materials, and consider your needs carefully.

☐ Check here if you need to ask your accountant about this subject.

Notes: _____

_____

_____

_____

_____

_____

56 Dependent Child Care

Under a cafeteria plan, many employers offer the option of reducing your salary by the amount of your child or dependent care expense. The money so diverted is not taxable income. Generally, your child must be younger than 13, or your disabled dependent, for you to qualify for this tax-free set-aside.

The IRS allows you to exclude up to $5,000 per year for dependent care, unless you or your spouse earn less than that. If that's the case, you are limited to excluding that lesser amount.

If you choose this option, you cannot take the child care credit on your tax return. You will want to consider the full consequences of your choice before you make it. If you are in at least the 28 percent tax bracket, the exclusion will likely save you more than with the child care credit, even if your state also offers a credit.

☐ Check here if you need to ask your accountant about this subject.

Notes: _____

_____

_____

_____

_____

_____

_____

57 Health Insurance

There's no telling at this writing what the health insurance situation could be, although someday it may change dramatically. Your employer will probably send around a fat memo when the dust settles, and there is always CNN. Stay tuned.

Just the same, here are some reckless predictions. Probably, your health expenses, including your insurance premiums, will remain deductible. Maybe you will still have to exclude 7.5 percent of your AGI from your deduction. The self-employed partners and those with 2 percent or more interest in S corporations may still have to include insurance premiums paid by the company as personal income. They may get to deduct 25 percent (or maybe 100 percent) of these premiums without being subject to the 7.5 percent AGI limit. Or maybe not. What a headache!

❑ Check here if you need to ask your accountant about this subject.

Notes: _____

_____

_____

_____

_____

_____

58 Other Fringe Benefits

Employee benefits are as good for your employer as they are for you. A healthy, cared-for employee is an asset to the company, and a good benefits package lures the best employees. You are not taxed on your benefits in most cases, and you get a little more for your efforts.

Your nontaxable fringe benefits may include: group term life insurance (up to $50,000); medical insurance; parking; employee discounts; noncash holiday gifts; and other de minimis fringes. You pay no taxes on these benefits, and you have a bit more disposable income, while your employer pays no FICA on your benefits. Everyone is ahead.

Some benefits are partly taxable, but may still be worthwhile. Group term life insurance premiums paid by your employer are not taxable to you, provided your coverage doesn't exceed $50,000. Taxable coverage in excess of $50,000 may also carry an advantage, since it is valued according to a low-cost formula.

☐ Check here if you need to ask your accountant about this subject.

Notes: _____

_____

_____

_____

_____

_____

59 Abandoned Spouse Rule

Divorce is difficult enough, and tax considerations can add an intense irritation to the mix. Still, decisions must be made. Often, couples facing divorce are loathe to file jointly, but neither can file as single until divorce is final. Both can file as married filing separately, but certain rules can increase friction already present. If one itemizes, then both must. A number of potential credits are lost. And the primary wage earner usually falls into a higher tax bracket. Although a joint return may lower your tax bracket, you then become liable for your spouse's tax. Carefully consider all ramifications before agreeing to a particular filing status. The tax law takes precedence over how your divorce decree may divide the tax liability.

There is another potential option for couples with children. If you are separated for the last six months of the tax year, don't file a joint return, and pay the majority of your housekeeping costs for a home that is also your child's home for more than half the year, you can file as Head of Household (HOH). This is permitted under the Abandoned Spouse Rule. If both partners meet the qualifications, both may file as HOH.

This option allows several additional credits over married filing separately. It also lowers certain marginal tax rates. The HOH filer can take the standard deduction even if the spouse itemizes, and the standard deduction is higher than for filing married and separately.

❑ Check here if you need to ask your accountant about this subject.

Notes: _____

_____

_____

_____

_____

PERSONAL TIP
60 Division Of Property

Here's where things often get lively. Aside from fairness, a divorcing couple's concerns are often emotional, and may at times provoke them to lay claims for other than financial reasons. When the dust settles, though, there can be considerable tax consequences to a property division.

A sensible plan is for the partner in the lower tax bracket to receive the property that has most appreciated in value. Any property transferred does so tax-free, but when it is sold the full gain is taxable. The partner in the lower bracket will realize a greater net return from a sale. So, don't just look at the current fair market value of the property to be divided. Also consider future taxable gains that will reduce the amount you ultimately receive.

These rules changed in 1984. If you divorced before that, your gain is only that accumulated since the division, and only that gain is taxable to you.

☐ Check here if you need to ask your accountant about this subject.

Notes: _____

_____

_____

PERSONAL TIP 61 — Qualified Domestic Relations Order (QDRO)

At best, a divorcing couple looks forward to new beginnings. In their difficult preparations to part, they sometimes neglect their retirement funds. Some even think their IRAs, 401(k)s, Keoghs, and other plans are not subject to division of property, which can be a costly error. When those funds are needed for support or property division payments, the court's help is needed to avoid penalties for early withdrawal.

The court can issue a Qualified Domestic Relations Order, which directs a retirement fund's administrator to pay specific amounts to the former spouse or children. Payments under the order are exempt from early withdrawal penalties. The payee spouse may defer tax on the payments by rolling them over into an IRA within 60 days of receipt.

Bear in mind that payments made to a child are taxed to the payer, though they are still exempt from penalties for early withdrawal.

☐ Check here if you need to ask your accountant about this subject.

Notes: _____

_____

_____

_____

_____

_____

Reclassify Child Support

As much as a divorcing couple may want to stay out of each other's lives, some issues may continue to require discussion, especially if they have children. The rules regarding tax treatment of child support and alimony seem ready-made to encourage lively disagreement. The following is a suggested approach that may save time and feelings, provided the parties agree that tax reduction is their common goal.

Child support is excluded from the recipient's taxable income, and the payer cannot deduct it. Conversely, alimony is included in the recipient's taxable income, and the payer can deduct it. You can see the battle lines forming, can't you?

Try this truce. The payer of support is usually in a higher tax bracket than is the recipient. Since child support isn't a deductible expense, and alimony is taxable income, child support will produce a higher total tax obligation than will alimony. Even more happily, support classified as alimony can be a larger amount than child support and actually save both parties money. The appropriate increase in payments under this reclassification depends on the parties' tax rates. Get some help with the figures if you need it, maybe not from a relative. Why ask for trouble?

☐ Check here if you need to ask your accountant about this subject.

Notes: _____

_____

_____

_____

_____

_____

Tax-Related Professional Advice

Divorce is expensive enough. While both parties would like to recover emotionally and financially as quickly as possible, your legal expenses from a divorce are not generally deductible.

However, you can deduct that portion of your lawyer's and accountant's fees that relate to tax advice. Potential future gain from property division, taxability of alimony and child support, and distribution of retirement plans are tax issues. Ask your divorce attorney to provide you with itemized bills so that you can break out the deductible portion of your legal costs.

If you later contest the division of taxable income (the amount of alimony, for instance) in your divorce decree, your legal fees may be largely or entirely deductible. Fees paid to contest other items in your decree will not be deductible.

❑ Check here if you need to ask your accountant about this subject.

Notes: _____

_____

_____

_____

_____

_____

Home: A Loan

One mortgage can be so much fun, it may not be too long before you're ready for another one, especially if you can get a better interest rate. But you may wish to take on additional debt to improve your home and take further tax advantages.

If you refinance your home to make substantial improvements, the points you pay should be deductible immediately. If you simply refinance to improve your loan rate, you must deduct points over the life of the loan.

If you refinance, you can generally deduct the remaining points in that year, because you have in essence paid off the original loan. This applies to any mortgage you pay off early, whether on your first or second home, so long as you have been deducting monthly portions of your points paid. (This may not apply if your loan is simply modified by the existing lender.)

☐ Check here if you need to ask your accountant about this subject.

Notes: _____

_____

_____

_____

_____

_____

Home: A Loan (Part 2)

Once, you could take a trip on the interest deductions gathered from credit card loans, education loans, and auto loans. These days, it seems taxpayers have been abandoned to the attic, and the IRS must be doing Disneyland on the money from disallowed deductions.

But there is one way you can still get cash relief and tax relief. You can take a loan against the home equity you've accumulated and deduct the interest, and then pay off some of those nondeductible interest loans. Or think before you spend.

You can use the proceeds of your home equity loan for education, a car, or for any other purpose, and still deduct the interest.

There are limits. Only the interest on a loan equal to or less than your equity is deductible, up to a loan maximum of $100,000. Don't forget that your home, as collateral, could be lost if you don't keep up the payments.

❏ Check here if you need to ask your accountant about this subject.

Notes: _____

_____

_____

_____

_____

Home Mortgage Interest – Second Home

PERSONAL TIP 66

No doubt you know you can deduct the interest on your primary home. You can also deduct interest from your vacation condo. So, what are the requirements for a secondary home?

A home must offer a place to sleep, a toilet, and cooking facilities. Your condo, vacation home, mobile home, travel trailer, recreational vehicle, and some boats qualify as a home. You can deduct the interest from your weekend cottage plus the interest from your primary residence if you meet a few guidelines.

Your loans from both primary and secondary residences cannot exceed $1,000,000. This includes monies used to improve the two homes. If you are renting the second home to help pay the mortgage, you must personally use the second home for 14 days or 10 percent of the rental days, whichever is more, in order to claim residence interest.

If you have more than one secondary home, consider which home loans will give you the greatest deduction. The IRS allows you to select a different secondary home each year, as long as the total amount of the loans does not exceed $1,000,000.

Consult with your accountant about reclassifying additional homes as rentals or business property.

☐ Check here if you need to ask your accountant about this subject.

Notes: _____

_____

_____

_____

_____

_____

67 Points And Closing Costs

When you are ready to join the company of the landed gentry, to mow your own lawn and fix your own plumbing, to put a nail in any wall you please, you can reap an immediate tax advantage by paying points. Points are interest payments on your mortgage, which may be fully deductible in the year paid. The additional advantage to paying points is that your mortgage rate is reduced over the life of the loan.

Point payments are only deductible if the loan is secured by your home, if the loan is for purchase or improvement of your primary home, and if points are for the use of money (and not a service charge). Otherwise, though paying points will still reduce your mortgage rate, you may only deduct those points in monthly increments over the life of the loan.

While closing costs are not generally deductible, they do add to the cost basis of your home, and so will reduce your gain when it's time to sell. A lesser gain will produce a smaller tax obligation, so keep track of all those costs.

☐ Check here if you need to ask your accountant about this subject.

Notes: _____

_____

_____

_____

_____

_____

Losses From Selling Your Home

Sooner or later, someone tells every one of us that real estate is the most reliable investment. You've heard it. Maybe that's why you bought your home and why you're so amazed if it's declining in value. If that's the case, you may feel boxed in. You can't deduct a loss on the sale of your home, which makes a sale seem financially impossible.

A way out may be to move out and rent your home, or possibly stay and convert part of your home to business use. For the years your home produces income, you can claim a depreciation deduction. If your home is now rental property, you may be able to deduct any annual operating loss. When you sell your home, you can claim a business loss, but that loss will be netted against the total of your depreciation over the years.

Of course, if your home increases in value after you begin renting, you could have a gain on the sale. Then you would pay tax on the gain, but that's not all bad, since you would be getting some money.

☐ Check here if you need to ask your accountant about this subject.

Notes: _____

_____

_____

_____

_____

_____

An Office In Your Home

What could be more pleasant than to sit down to work in your pajamas, your slippered feet up on your desk, your loyal dog by your side? If you can get anything done like that, and your employer goes for it, a home office can be a little slice of paradise and a great tax saver. The same is true for your own business at home.

You must use space in your home exclusively for business on a regular basis in order to take business deductions. It is not enough to take business calls or do administrative work at home for a business conducted elsewhere. The best rule of thumb is that your home must be your most important business location (for instance, produce the bulk of your income from the relevant business), and the majority of your work time must be spent at home.

Deductible items include the appropriate percentage of your insurance, home repairs, and utilities. Improvements to your office are fully deductible so long as they relate to the conduct of business. If you own your home, you can depreciate the portion you use for business. If you rent, you can deduct a portion of your rent.

Your home office deductions cannot exceed your income from the business. You can carry excess deductions forward to future years. However, depreciating part of your home as an office can have adverse consequences later. When you sell your home, any gain on the business portion cannot be rolled over into the purchase of a new home.

☐ Check here if you need to ask your accountant about this subject.

Notes: _____

_____

_____

_____

_____

_____

One-Time Exclusion On The Sale Of Your Home

The kids are finally out of the house, and you've dropped your last dollar in the office hospitality fund. You're a free, mighty wanderer! Visions of the open road, white sand, and endless room service beckon.

You'll turn that engine over and let the wind whisper where you're bound.

Or maybe you'll go on being sensible. Either way, you may well want to unload the dear old dustcatcher you've called home all these years. If you're 55 or older, selling your home can feather your nest egg nicely. The IRS allows you to exclude from tax your first $125,000 of gain from the sale.

There are rules. You must have lived in and owned your home for at least three of the last five years. You cannot exclude gain on the part of your home you rent or use for business. If you co-own, only one of you need be 55. You may make this exclusion only once in your life, even if your gain is less than $125,000. This one-time rule applies to you and your spouse, together and separately. If you take a new spouse and either of you has taken the exclusion, neither of you can again.

☐ Check here if you need to ask your accountant about this subject.

Notes: _____

_____

_____

_____

_____

Purchasing A Second House

You know how it can be. You don't want to stay home, and you don't want to go out. The happy solution, if you can manage it, is a second home, maybe even on the beach or in the piney woods. If you take the plunge, remember that tax rules for a second home are different.

Interest on a second home is deductible if it's a qualified residential mortgage. Points paid on a loan for a second home are not immediately deductible, so it may be to your advantage not to pay points and instead take the higher interest rate. If you choose to pay points to get the lower rate, remember, for the life of the loan, you can only deduct prorated monthly portions of your points paid.

You can still deduct your property taxes for your second home. You can also save considerable money by renting the place for part of the year and deducting the appropriate portion of the upkeep, insurance, and utility costs. Different methods of figuring these deductions apply, but you must rent out the place more than 14 days of the year to take any of them. If you use the place yourself less than 14 days or 10 percent of your rental days, you can even claim a rental property loss. Consult your accountant. Maybe he needs a vacation.

If you rent your home (or vacation home) for less than 15 days, you don't have to report the rental income. So, if your city holds some event which draws throngs of visitors, you can rent out your home for a short period and pocket the money free of tax.

☐ Check here if you need to ask your accountant about this subject.

Notes: _____

_____

_____

_____

_____

Rollovers From Selling Your Home

An investment that pays off is a thing of beauty, and many people look forward eagerly to the day they sell their home for a sizeable profit. When the day comes, though, the tax man can show up and spoil the party. When you sell your home, your gain is fully taxable – with one convenient exception, that is.

You can roll over your gain into the purchase of a new home and avoid taxation for now. Sensible as ever, Congress realized that most people could not both pay tax and buy a new home, so they allowed for this rollover.

There are some rules. Both homes must be your primary residence (though not at the same time, naturally). The price of your new home must be at least equal to your old home's sale price, minus your expenses for preparing it for sale. (Otherwise, you will owe tax on part of your gain.) You must move into your new home within the two years before or the two years after you sell your old home. That is, you must actually live in your new home during part of those four years.

☐ Check here if you need to ask your accountant about this subject.

Notes: _____

_____

_____

_____

_____

_____

73 Household Help

Nannygate wasn't much, as scandals go, but it sent some taxpayers scurrying to see if they were in compliance with the law. The new law, effective in 1994, set a $1,000 annual wage threshold for FICA taxes paid on domestics. The law does not apply to an employee of a service contracted by your household, or to someone who is not your household employee. Certain employees under age 18, such as babysitters and yard workers, may be exempt.

If FICA tax has already been paid on an employee's 1994 wages that are less than $1,000, both the employer and employee will be entitled to refunds in 1995. (FICA on wages paid in 1994 should have been paid quarterly with Form 942.)

Starting in 1996, FICA tax will be due on an employer's 1040 for wages paid to employees in 1995.

☐ Check here if you need to ask your accountant about this subject.

Notes: _____

_____

_____

_____

_____

_____

PERSONAL TIP 74

Exemptions For Family Members

There's nothing sweeter than the day you drag out the bankroll to bail Junior out on the rent, and he says, "No thanks, I'll take care of it." He's growing up, moving on, and your bittersweet smile glows, until tax time brings you to your senses. The little loved one has taken his personal exemption with him, and you're stuck for taxes you haven't paid in years!

Don't panic yet; maybe you can still qualify him as a dependent. Junior might still meet the IRS definition of a dependent. (In part, he must be a relative for whom you pay more than half his support, and either be a full-time student under 24 or have less than about $2,500 in income for the year.) In this case, it could be to his advantage as well as yours for you to qualify to claim his exemption. Since you are in the higher tax bracket, you will reap more savings. You may want to pass along the savings Junior gave up with his exemption and keep the remainder for yourself. But remember, as exemptions are phased out for upper-income taxpayers, you may not benefit at all if your income is too high.

The same strategy can work with another relative, such as your parent, for whom you provide more than half the support. Some people get understandably rankled at the suggestion that they are 'dependent,' so approach the subject tactfully.

☐ Check here if you need to ask your accountant about this subject.

Notes: _____

_____

_____

_____

_____

_____

75 Multiple Support Agreements

Family members sometimes share the support of a relative, which eases everyone's burden. Unfortunately, if none of the parties pays more than half the support, the personal exemption remains with the dependent relative, who may not have the income to benefit by it.

A solution is to agree among the parties to designate one member to take the dependent exemption. Others who pay at least 10 percent of support must file Form 2120 to relinquish claim to the exemption. The parties can take turns taking the exemption year to year, which will eventually save everyone money.

If you are a high-income taxpayer, remember that you may not benefit due to the exemption phase out.

☐ Check here if you need to ask your accountant about this subject.

Notes: _____

_____

_____

_____

_____

_____

The Kiddie Tax

Children under 14 pay no tax at all on their first $600 in unearned income, and 15 percent on the next $600. Then, however, the "Kiddie Tax" kicks in.

The "Kiddie Tax" is at the parents' highest marginal tax rate, and it is applied to unearned income over $1,200 for children under 14. Several methods are available to avoid the "Kiddie Tax." Shift the child's investments to tax-free securities or to investments that defer taxes until the child's 14th birthday. Cover the child with a life insurance policy that shelters current income from tax.

Or divide your child's income with a special trust. Undistributed income is taxed to the trust, and only distributed income is taxed to the child. Be aware that at majority (age 21) the child will receive all principal and accumulated earnings, which may then have tax consequences.

☐ Check here if you need to ask your accountant about this subject.

Notes: _____

_____

_____

_____

_____

_____

77 AMT Planning

Congress is forever axing one bunch of deductions and adding others. And for those of us who are doing well, they've found a way to give us deductions and then, sometimes, take them away. It's the Alternative Minimum Tax (AMT), a separate tax computing system applied to upper-income taxpayers to ensure they don't escape tax liability through large deductions. Even if you don't think of yourself as "upper income," you may be subject to AMT, or at least have to do some calculations.

First, you have to figure your taxes as if you get to take all of your regular deductions. Then, separately, you must add certain deductions back into your taxable income. Subtract your AMT exemption from that amount and determine your AMT. You owe the greater amount of tax.

The first $175,000 of AMT income is taxed at 26 percent. Any excess is taxed at 28 percent. Keep in mind that income above certain maximums reduces the AMT exemption.

If AMT applies to you, certain strategies can reduce your tax. You can defer deductions to later years rather than accelerating them. If you already know you will be subject to AMT this year, consider accelerating income. It could be taxed at the AMT rate, which is lower than your regular rate. Certain elections may reduce your AMT. Ask your accountant for more information.

❏ Check here if you need to ask your accountant about this subject.
Notes: _____
_____
_____
_____
_____
_____
_____

AMT Credits

Sure, alternative minimum tax (AMT) is complicated, but it's just a warm-up for the AMT credit you may be able to take in subsequent years. If you must pay AMT, and in a later year your regular tax exceeds your AMT, certain deductions can allow you a credit. The computations involved can be mind-numbing, but the credit can be worth the pain.

The most common source of a credit is depreciation on business and rental property. AMT depreciation schedules exceed depreciation under regular tax in later years. An AMT taxpayer who later pays regular tax and therefore doesn't benefit from AMT depreciation can take a credit for the lost depreciation.

This credit does not apply to every deduction disallowed under the AMT. You will want to be sure that credits you claim are allowable. Your accountant can explain AMT, credits, and planning to you.

☐ Check here if you need to ask your accountant about this subject.

Notes: _____

_____

_____

_____

_____

_____

79 Amortizing Intangibles

It used to be that some of the assets you acquired when you purchased a business could not be amortized on your return. Concrete assets were valued as part of the purchase price and could be deducted according to the appropriate schedules. But intangible assets, like trademarks, customer lists, and goodwill often could not be amortized, even though they had value. This was because generally a useful life could not be determined.

The 1993 Revenue Reconciliation Act changed all that. Generally, intangibles acquired after August 10, 1993, now must be amortized over 15 years. And capitalized costs of developing and registering a franchise, trademark, or trade name can also be amortized over 15 years. This 15-year period also applies to noncompete agreements. Although you are now assured of a deduction for your entire asset purchase, you have generally lost the ability to agree on shorter asset lives.

It's still important to look at the mix of assets purchased. And if you purchased intangibles, or entered into an agreement to do so, between July 25, 1991, and Aug. 10, 1993, you may benefit from an available election.

☐ Check here if you need to ask your accountant about this subject.

Notes: _____

_____

_____

_____

_____

_____

Employee vs. Independent Contractor: Which Are You? Which Should You Hire?

Many businesses and professionals see advantages in contract labor over formal employment. A business avoids payroll taxes and the related insurance and benefit costs. And, unlike an employee, a contractor can deduct all of her related expenses rather than reducing them by 2 percent of her AGI. And, she can often go to work in sweats.

It's not enough, however, to simply agree that certain work is contract labor. The IRS is keeping its beady eye on those who claim to be independent contractors, and has developed guidelines to determine whether their work is in fact contract labor. You may hear of a list called the "20 Common Law Factors." It's based on IRS rulings and case law.

Essentially, the determination is based on who controls the work. An independent contractor sets her own hours and chooses where and how she works. She is paid by the job, which stands apart from the client's regular operations. She receives little or no training or supervision, and is not generally required to submit reports. She has a variety of clients at the same time, and works full time for none of them. Her services are generally available to the public. None of these guidelines decides the question alone, since contract work is so varied. But a contractor should arrange her work life to comply with them as much as possible, in case the IRS raises the question.

☐ Check here if you need to ask your accountant about this subject.

Notes: _____

_____

_____

_____

_____

_____

81 Inventory: Which Method Is Best? Can You Change Your System?

What could be more straightforward than buying and selling? And what could be more exasperating than tracking the varying age and cost of inventory against its changing sales price? Yet, the one requires the other, especially when tax time comes.

You may find it difficult or impossible to identify the specific inventory you've sold. It somewhat simplifies matters that the IRS has specifically approved only two inventory methods for intermingled merchandise, FIFO and LIFO. FIFO (first-in, first-out) assumes that you sell your oldest merchandise first. LIFO (last-in, first-out) assumes that you sell your most recently purchased merchandise first. If your inventory costs generally rise, you have the advantage with LIFO of deducting your highest costs against sales, and may, in fact, never sell down to your least expensive inventory. So, LIFO may offer a big tax advantage.

LIFO isn't for everyone, though. To use LIFO, you must value your inventory at its actual cost, and you must use LIFO in your reports to shareholders, partners, and lenders. The tax advantage may not impress these parties as much as your smaller bottom line under LIFO.

You may use some other inventory system so long as it accurately reflects your income according to appropriate accounting practices. One option for small businesses is "simplified dollar-value LIFO," in which the cost of equivalent goods is averaged. But don't try to puzzle out the options yourself. This decision will have a powerful influence on your viability, and your accountant can show you where your advantages lie. Changing your inventory system usually requires application to the IRS and complex tax adjustments.

❑ Check here if you need to ask your accountant about this subject.

Notes: _____

_____

_____

82 New Business Equipment

Thank heavens, and the IRS, for depreciation! If only your blessing, that is, deduction, could be larger. Well, there is an alternative deduction that may save you big money at tax time.

If you purchase new equipment or furniture during the year, you can elect to deduct the full cost up to a $17,500 maximum, rather than spreading your expense out over years of depreciation. In this way, you can ease at once the hit of a major purchase.

You may choose each year whether to depreciate or deduct your equipment purchases, though once you file, you cannot change your mind regarding that purchase. To qualify for the purchase deduction, you must have business income. Also, if your equipment purchases total more than $200,000 for the year, your maximum expense deduction is reduced. By planning your qualifying purchases before year-end, you can maximize your write-off.

☐ Check here if you need to ask your accountant about this subject.

Notes: _____

_____

_____

_____

_____

_____

83 Salaries: How Much Is Enough?

What would you think if the IRS charged that your salary is unreasonably low? A great bunch of public servants, right? Probably not. The IRS has its eye on S corporations that pay employee-shareholders small salaries combined with large distributions to avoid FICA payments on the latter. It's not legal, unless you can prove your salary is "reasonable" under the law. Better to avoid the legal expense and tax penalties and take an appropriate salary.

Some regular (C) corporations are having the opposite problem. Upper-level salaries are routinely examined by the IRS to determine if they are unreasonably large. The IRS asserts in such cases that the excess is actually dividends and therefore not deductible by the corporation. If you look forward to such a problem, compensation planning through appropriate formulas and documentation can help establish support for your large salary according to factors considered by the IRS. The IRS is less likely to disallow such demonstrable compensation.

☐ Check here if you need to ask your accountant about this subject.

Notes: _____

_____

_____

_____

_____

_____

84 Supplies Before Year-End

Year-end sales come but once a year, and the bargains you can find as a consumer may have parallels in your business. Even if you don't find a price break in supplies or equipment, you might consider stocking up anyway, especially at the end of a good year, when you have a considerable vulnerability to a tax bite.

Protect one good year by investing in the next. Your deduction for large end-of-year purchases or expense payments can protect your current profits, and may also protect your margin from a future supplies price increase.

Don't overdo it, though. You don't want to warehouse two years' worth of stationery that may become unusable. Talk to your accountant.

☐ Check here if you need to ask your accountant about this subject.

Notes: _____

_____

_____

_____

_____

_____

Structuring Your Company

Who said that smile on your face was too big as you waved adieu to your old employer? Before you take on your first clients, consult your accountant on the best tax structure for your company.

C corporations are taxed as separate entities and have certain tax obligations all their own. The corporation pays taxes, and you'll pay taxes as an employee. Investors are taxed on dividends received. C corporations can offer more fringe benefits, but also receive more IRS scrutiny regarding salaries and accumulated earnings.

You can usually avoid the corporate level of tax and may be more likely to find outside investors if you're an S corporation. But you'll face more restrictions. An S corporation is limited to 35 shareholders, none of whom may be corporations or nonresidents.

An S corporation may issue only one class of stock, and is barred from certain businesses, like insurance and banking.

Partnerships avoid corporate double taxation. In a sole proprietorship, your personal return is your business return. Still, if you risk substantial liability in your business, you may consider some form of incorporation to protect your personal assets.

Limited Liability Companies (LLCs) and Limited Liability Partnerships (LLPs) are fairly new and offer plenty of advantages. You are taxed as a partnership, you have flexibility to include many types of owners, and you limit your liabilities. If you are part owner of an LLP, you are called a "partner." In an LLC, you'll call yourself a "member."

☐ Check here if you need to ask your accountant about this subject.

Notes: _____

_____

_____

_____

_____

Transportation And Expense Plans That Qualify

A company may best serve itself and its employees by instituting what's called an "accountable plan" for expense reimbursements. Employees who travel during the day submit mileage logs or actual expense receipts, and the employer reimburses them at the standard mileage rate or for the expenses. The company can deduct the full reimbursements, and the employees don't report the reimbursements as income or deduct any expenses. It's a wash to the employees.

Under a "nonaccountable plan," employees don't report expenses to the employer, and the employer may pay only a flat expense allowance. An employee can lose in this arrangement. The reimbursement or allowance is included on his W-2 as income, but his expenses, as miscellaneous itemized deductions, are subject to the 2 percent of AGI limit. It's not a wash. The employer may owe FICA on the reimbursements and lose as well.

☐ Check here if you need to ask your accountant about this subject.

Notes: _____

_____

_____

_____

_____

_____

Travel And Entertainment

The IRS keeps one of its beadiest eyes on travel and entertainment expense deductions. And the limits keep getting more severe. The most recent changes are that meal and entertainment deductions are limited to 50 percent of cost for tax years beginning after Dec. 31, 1993. Additionally, most club dues paid after Dec. 31, 1993, are not deductible.

Be sure your records are adequate for the rules, and think through your expenses in these areas. To protect your deductions, ask yourself these questions: Are gifts incorrectly recorded as entertainment? Are subscriptions incorrectly recorded as dues? Are fully deductible expenses like employee recreation incorrectly recorded as meals and entertainment?

If you will be working away from home for a while, or you are planning an overseas business trip, ask your accountant about the rules. The duration of a temporary assignment can affect its deductibility. The length of your foreign trip, and what you do there, can affect your deduction, too. A matter as small as the number of days between your business meetings can make a great difference at tax time.

☐ Check here if you need to ask your accountant about this subject.

Notes: _____

_____

_____

_____

_____

_____

88   Like-Kind Exchanges

Every now and then, an investor ends up with more property or business than can be managed. If that's your problem, you may want to dispose of your investment without having to recognize the gain. It's the oldest method of economic exchange, and you can use it to defer your gain.

Exchange the property solely for "like-kind" property, and no gain need be recognized. Whether property qualifies as like-kind depends on the nature of the property, not the value or quality. Real estate for real estate, for instance, works as a like-kind exchange.

If you receive anything in addition to the property, such as cash, or you are relieved of any liabilities, you must recognize the gain up to the value of this additional amount you received.

Consider three points before making any like-kind exchanges.

• Any gain you defer reduces the base value of the replacement property by that amount.

• While you don't have to recognize the gain, you can't recognize the loss, either.

• Some property, such as inventory and stock, does not qualify as eligible like-kind property.

Be sure you consult your accountant about opportunities and details before completing any like-kind exchanges.

☐ Check here if you need to ask your accountant about this subject.

Notes: _____

_____

_____

_____

_____

_____

Sell Your Business Through A Tax-Free Reorganization

You've dedicated a large part of your life to building your business from scratch. Now, you're ready to retire and you've found a buyer who will continue to operate your business with the same integrity.

Suddenly, it seems the IRS is coming after the appreciation on your business with the force of a rabid badger. What can you do to dispose of your business and avoid the tremendous capital gain?

While you can't avoid the gain completely, you can defer it into years where you can manage the tax liability more easily. Rather than sell your business to an acquiring company for cash, ask for stock instead. If you receive stock in the acquiring company as part of a tax-free reorganization, no gain is recognized by the corporation. Plus, you won't have to recognize any gain until you sell the stock.

Recognize the gain at your discretion. You can sell all at once or sell piece by piece so long as you have no prior commitment to sell at the time of reorganization.

❏ Check here if you need to ask your accountant about this subject.

Notes: _____

_____

_____

_____

_____

_____

90 Americans With Disabilities Act

A sound tax strategy will certainly benefit your business, but the best strategy is still to find and secure more business. The last thing you need is an office inaccessible to your customers. Customers with disabilities will go elsewhere if your place of business is not accessible. Two federal laws require you to provide access, which will certainly improve your prospective customer base.

The law also allows deductions for the cost of compliance. You may get a credit of up to $5,000 for costs to comply with the Americans with Disabilities Act, and a deduction of up to $15,000 to comply with the Architectural and Transportation Barrier Removal Act.

☐ Check here if you need to ask your accountant about this subject.

Notes: _____

_____

_____

_____

_____

_____

Rebuilding Old Buildings

It's not only chic to renovate an old building for use. You can find great tax advantages in an antique structure. If a building is on the National Register of Historic Places or in a Registered Historic District, you can deduct 20 percent of the renovation costs from your tax bill.

A similar 10 percent Rehabilitation Credit applies to renovations to buildings first used before 1936. For these nonhistoric buildings, the law says that 75 percent of the original exterior walls and interior framework must be retained for the tax credit to apply. Consult with your accountant and your contractor before beginning work to be certain you can receive the credit.

❑ Check here if you need to ask your accountant about this subject.

Notes: _____

_____

_____

_____

_____

_____

Empowerment Zones: Are You In One?

Certainly by now you know. If your community applied and was chosen as one of the 104 Federal Empowerment Zones (EZ) in Enterprise Cities (EC) for this year, you'll find a hot debate over how to use the federal funds. Distressed areas of pervasive poverty and unemployment can expect additional money for social services, law enforcement, and housing construction and rehabilitation.

Local businesspeople will have favorable investment and taxation policies to look into. An eligible business in the zone can get a federal loan at preferred rates or secure a private loan with federal leverage. Enterprise communities (EC) are eligible for tax-exempt facility bonds for certain private businesses. A business in an EZ can get a wage and training credit on taxes up to $3,000 per employee who lives in the zone. Zone businesses can qualify for a higher limit on their expense deductions, and their investors may be eligible for a 50 percent exclusion of capital gains.

And there's more. If your business is in an EC or EZ, or if you conduct business in one, have your accountant explore your options. If you are not, and your area might qualify, watch for the possible reinstatement or expansion of the program next year. Think about getting involved in the application process, for your community as well as for yourself.

☐ Check here if you need to ask your accountant about this subject.

Notes: _____

_____

_____

_____

_____

_____

93 Low-Income Housing Credit

The law encourages the new construction of low-income housing. As an investor or builder, you can reduce your tax bill through an annual credit of approximately 9 percent of qualified new construction costs. The credit is granted for 10 consecutive years, which amounts to substantial tax savings. Some or all of the credit can be taken against tax on any type of income, and unused credit can be carried forward. For federally subsidized construction, and even for acquisition of existing housing, there is a similar credit of approximately 4 percent.

Keep in mind that low-income housing is not a high-yield investment, though you could well see a positive cash flow. Even if you don't, any passive losses generated can offset passive gain from other sources. And you will still get that credit. (The credit is not treated as passive income up to a certain dollar amount.)

The laws regarding compliance are complex and exhaustive, so secure competent advice and counsel before committing yourself to a long-term investment. Stability is essential, as the development must remain in compliance with regulations for 15 years or your tax credit is subject to recapture.

❑ Check here if you need to ask your accountant about this subject.

Notes: _____

_____

_____

_____

_____

_____

Reinstated Research And Development Credits

If you missed this one last year, you've got another chance. The Federal 20% Research and Development Credit was reinstated retroactively to June 30, 1992, and expires June 30, 1995. If your firm has done or paid for qualified research, you may benefit from filing amended returns or claiming the credit this year.

The credit applies to businesses whose R&D expenses in the tax year are larger than the average expenses for the preceding three years. Start-up businesses get a significant break in the way their credit is figured.

We're not talking rocket science here. A generous variety of information-gathering activities and their attendant wages and expenses is eligible. If you did some business-related inquiry, and it cost you money, have your accountant work up your eligibility. And watch for a possible extension of the credit into the future.

☐ Check here if you need to ask your accountant about this subject.

Notes: _____

_____

_____

_____

_____

_____

State Incentive Credits

We've just discussed a number of tax credits offered by the federal government. Many state governments, not to be outdone, offer a few tax credits of their own. While the credits available, if any, vary from state to state, some of the more common credits are as follows: enterprise zone credits for operating your business in certain geographical areas, business development and expansion credits for adding new employees and facilities, and various other credits similar to the ones on the federal level. Your accountant can help you determine which credits apply in your situation.

☐ Check here if you need to ask your accountant about this subject.

Notes: _____

_____

_____

_____

_____

_____